Sorted in 30 days

FINDING LOVE

THIS IS A CARLTON BOOK

This edition published by
Carlton Books Limited 2002
20 Mortimer Street
London W1T 3JW

A CIP catalogue record for this book
is available from the British Library
ISBN 1 84222 507 3

Printed and bound in Dubai

Editorial Manager:
Judith More
Art Director:
Penny Stock
Senior Art Editor:
Barbara Zuñiga
Executive Editor:
Zia Mattocks
Design:
LewisHallam
Editors:
Siobhán O'Connor
and Libby Willis
Production Controller:
Janette Burgin
Illustrations:
Lucy Truman

Sorted in 30 days

FINDING LOVE

how to find the perfect partner
in just one month

caro handley

CARLTON
BOOKS

Contents

Introduction

You deserve to find real love. You deserve a warm, exciting, funny, sexy, generous, committed and loving relationship with a man who appreciates, respects and loves you.

It doesn't matter how old or young you are, whether you've been in lots of relationships or none at all, whether you always end it or he does, whether you rush in or go at snail's pace, whether you know why you haven't found love so far or you don't have a clue – none of these things matters. Love is still only an arm's reach away from you.

All that is truly important is that you know that you want love and that you are willing to put some time and energy into finding it and bringing it into your life.

Finding love isn't just a question of luck. You can wait for it, like a princess in a tower waiting for her knight. Or you can make the changes, put in the effort and go out and find it. Which would you rather do? Wait, not knowing whether it will ever come? Or go out and find it, knowing that if you do you cannot fail.

If you're open and willing, I will show you, step by step, what you need to do. In 30 days you can transform your world and make changes you never imagined possible. The path to finding love is an exciting one and with each step you take you will feel love draw ever closer.

Decide to find love and let the adventure begin ...

Day One

ARE YOU READY?

You want a relationship, right? And not just any relationship – a fantastic one. An exciting, lasting, passionate and fun relationship with a man who's open, honest, understanding and supportive. Not to mention solvent, responsible and grown-up enough to have his own life pretty well sorted out.

Sounds good, doesn't it? You've waited long enough, made enough mistakes, kissed enough frogs – now you're ready for real love with the right person. And you're going to find it, if you're determined, brave and honest with yourself.

On day one it's time for the first step towards finding love, and that is to check just how ready you are. It's all very well being ready in principle. It's fine to talk about finding love, to wish, to hope and to dream. Being truly ready to take the first step, however, means being willing to take action, to make changes and to do things differently. That can feel uncomfortable and a little scary. Sometimes it's a lot easier just to go on talking about what you want, rather than actually doing what's needed to bring it into your life.

Today I want you to think about the following key points and to prepare yourself for the changes you're about to make in your life:

- Are you ready to shed your excuses, outdated beliefs and unhelpful attitudes that keep you stuck in the same old patterns and prevent you having what you want?
- Are you ready to think in new ways, adopt new beliefs and become the kind of person who can attract the love you want in your life?
- Are you ready to take action and to keep taking action until you succeed?
- Are you ready to be open to change, however uncomfortable it may feel, and to welcome new possibilities into your life?
- Are you ready to give love, to be loved and to share your life with another person?

Think hard about every one of these questions. What will it mean for you to share your space, your way of life, your inner thoughts and feelings? If you want to find real love, this is precisely what it will involve.

Exercise

Say to yourself out loud: 'I am ready for love.' See how it feels. Repeat this phrase throughout the day. Notice the prickles of excitement, the moments of fear and the shivers of anticipation it may evoke. When you can say it standing in front of a mirror and looking yourself right in the eye, meaning it with all your heart, you're ready to start the journey to the kind of relationship that you want.

You are ready for love and all that it will bring you

Day Two

REMOVING THE BLOCKS

Before you can go out and find love, you have to remove any blocks that you may have put in its path.

Imagine yourself looking out of the window at a beautiful little garden just across the road. There are lush green plants, exquisite flowers, a small pond with a waterfall, and in the middle a seat where you long to sit, soaking in the beauty and magic of the surroundings. To get there, however, you need to navigate a path that is littered with obstacles: concrete blocks, heaps of rubble, piles of rotting garbage and discarded pieces of machinery. It looks daunting, but you want to reach the garden so much that you set out to make your way past all the obstacles.

Some of the impediments are surprisingly easy to remove – you can simply lift them out of the way. Others are heavy and stubbornly refuse to be moved. You have to try harder, take a little longer. But in the end you do it. The path is clear and you make it to the garden.

The blocks in life are exactly the same as the obstacles on the way to the garden. Whether we put them there ourselves or whether other people have placed them in our way isn't important. Just say to yourself that any block, no matter how big or how heavy, can be removed.

What are the blocks on your path to finding love? You may know some straight away. Others may be harder to identify.

The blocks on your path to finding love could be lifestyle choices, attitudes, other people around you or the way you feel about yourself. You may not even have realized that there are blocks there. Now that you know they exist, you can work at identifying them and start to move them out of your way.

Here are some examples:

- You hardly ever go out because you hate parties, bars and clubs, so your chances of meeting someone are pretty low.
- You refuse to make having a relationship a priority and place more importance on everything else in your life.
- You allow your mum/dad/best friend to tell you who you should or shouldn't date.
- You go out with anyone who asks you just because you're so grateful to be asked. This means you often spend your time with men who are wrong for you.
- You don't go out with anyone because you're shy, convinced you're ugly or scared of getting involved.
- You'd rather talk about how lovely it would be to have a great relationship than DO anything about it.

Get the idea?

How do you move these blocks? By recognizing them, deciding to shift them and then taking the necessary steps to do this, whatever those may be. You may need to start accepting invitations, to prioritize finding a relationship, to ask your best friend to take more of a back seat in your love life or to start making choices that are right for you. You'll know what needs doing once you know what the blocks are.

Remove the blocks and let love into your life

Day Three

NO MORE EXCUSES

This is the day when you're going to clear out all the stale old excuses that you've been using for not having a great relationship. No matter how badly you may want a relationship, if it's not in your life now it's because you've been clinging to excuses for not having it. Before you can go ahead and find the right relationship, you have to spring-clean your mind of all the buts, ifs and maybes you've been using to avoid it.

Why do we use excuses? Because they are a way of keeping things safely as they are now. Even if you think you don't like things as they are now, the situation is what you're used to and so it's comfortable and familiar to stick with the status quo. Also, a part of you prefers it that way, the part that's scared of change and of the various challenges a relationship will bring – to know someone really intimately; to share your space, time and possessions; and to really open up to another person.

Dumping your excuses will mean pulling the rug out from under the reluctant part of yourself. It will give the green light to the bigger part of you that's excited about getting out there and finding the love you want and deserve.

What are your excuses?

Take a pen and piece of paper and spend five minutes writing down all the excuses you use to avoid a relationship. You should end up with between five and ten. Here are some favourite ones:

- I'm simply too busy to meet anyone ...
- My life's great as it is – a relationship would be just a nice extra.
- I'm always attracted to the wrong type.
- I'm still not over the big hurt.
- I've got to lose weight/give up smoking/move house first.
- I'm concentrating on my career at the moment.
- Whenever I meet someone I like, he's already taken.
- My hands are full with the kids/my mum/my sister.
- Men/women are always intimidated by my success.
- No one would want to take on someone as difficult as me.

Recognize anything? You may find some of your excuses listed here, or you may come up with completely different ones. Just be sure to get them all down on paper.

Well done! That's got them out into the open and labelled as what they are: excuses that stop you from having a fantastic relationship.

Now it's time to bin them, once and for all.

Exercise

Pick a quiet time to do this exercise. Make sure there won't be any interruptions, and lie or sit somewhere comfortable with your eyes closed:

Imagine that the excuses you've identified are hanging around your neck on chains, weighing you down like heavy stones. You can hardly move under the sheer weight of them and you're desperate to off-load the burden.

Gradually, with enormous effort, you manage to lift them, one by one, from your neck and drop them into a sack. When they're all off, you rub your stiff neck and stretch your aching back, then drag the sack across to a huge black pit. You shove the sack into the pit and watch it fall to the bottom

You then walk away and, as you do so, you feel your body lightening and your energy returning. Your shoulders straighten up and a sense of joy and excitement fills you until you want to run, dance and leap in the air. You're free.

Now open your eyes and savour the sense of freedom you have just created. This is your starting point, your launch pad for finding the relationship you want. You have a clean slate, a fresh start, a whole new beginning.

From now on, your old excuses are gone. They're hollow, empty and meaningless. If you find yourself resorting to any one of them again – to yourself or to anyone else – stop immediately and say to yourself:

'I am completely free to find the relationship I want'

Day Four

ROOT OUT NEGATIVE BELIEFS

Today you're going to look at your relationship beliefs and decide which ones are useful and which ones need changing.

We all gather beliefs as we grow up. Some come from our parents, some from family members, teachers and friends. Others come from what we see in the world around us. We take on certain beliefs and then behave as though they're absolute truths, rigid and unchangeable.

Once we have certain beliefs, we look for evidence to support them in the world around us. Every time you see, hear or read something that fits in with one of your beliefs, it confirms it for you even more deeply.

Your beliefs are incredibly powerful. They govern your thoughts, which in turn govern your actions.

In order to find the love you are looking for, you need to get rid of negative and unhelpful beliefs. If you don't, however hard you try, you won't attract the person you want into your life – or you'll make sure that you lose them as fast as possible. You'll then resort to your beliefs to justify what happened, simply compounding them and ingraining them more deeply into your attitudes to life and love . . .

You will tell yourself: 'I knew I couldn't hang on to someone nice' or 'No one wants to be with me'.

The wonderful thing about beliefs is that, far from being unalterable, they can in fact be changed in a remarkably short space of time. Although children may have little choice about what they're taught to believe, adults can choose their own beliefs. This means that the power for change is in your hands.

The first step is to identify the negative beliefs that have been holding you back. Take ten minutes to write down as many as you can. You may find some of your beliefs on the following list and you will almost certainly be able to come up with a few more of your own.

Here are some examples:

- I'm not attractive.
- Men/women find me boring/bossy/a wimp.
- I don't deserve love.
- I always get dumped.
- I grow bored with partners so quickly that I have to dump them.
- I make the wrong choices.
- No one would want me.
- I can find partners, but I can't keep them.
- I don't know how to let anyone get close to me.

Once you have finished your list, go through it and examine each of your beliefs. Are they really true? Or is each one something you have chosen to believe because of things that have happened in the past? Perhaps someone hurt you. Painful though that was, it hasn't been your only experience and needn't form the basis of your beliefs for the future. Perhaps a cruel remark stuck and became a rigidly held belief about yourself. But there will have been other, kind and appreciative remarks. Why stick with the nasty one?

Decide now that you will let these negative beliefs go and choose not to embrace them any longer. They are old, tired, burdensome and outdated.

Let go of negative beliefs and set yourself free

Day Five

CHOOSE YOUR NEW BELIEFS

Now that you've rooted out your longstanding negative and damaging beliefs, here comes the fun part – choosing the beliefs that you really want to have.

Before you begin it's important to recognize that you do already have plenty of useful, good and supportive beliefs, as well as those negative and restrictive old ones. So take a pen and piece of paper and spend ten minutes writing down all the positive beliefs you have about yourself and relationships. Here are some examples:

- **I'm trustworthy and loyal.**
- **I know a good person when I meet one.**
- **I'm fun to be with and good company.**
- **I'm generous.**
- **I'm great at sharing.**
- **I won't be put down or trampled upon.**
- **I pick myself up quickly after setbacks.**
- **I can talk about my feelings.**
- **I'm thoughtful and caring.**
- **It is possible to have a longlasting, fulfilling relationship.**

Pick the positive beliefs that apply to you and add as many others as you can think of. Don't hold back when it comes to praising yourself: list every good quality you believe you have – and have fun doing it. Are you surprised by how many there are? This only goes to show how we tend to tuck these beliefs away deep inside, instead of bringing them out and enjoying them.

Now it's time to choose some new beliefs, which will reinforce and support those you already hold. New beliefs can be taken up surprisingly quickly; in fact we often learn them instantly.

If you doubt this, simply bring to mind any fact you have read or heard in the past 24 hours. It could be something you heard on the television news or read in a newspaper or magazine. You believed it and it is now a part of your belief system – the way you shape and make sense of the world. Why did you believe it so easily? Because you trusted the source, you were open to the belief and it made sense to you. Teaching yourself to adhere to new beliefs can happen in the same way.

Exercise

Make a list of five new beliefs that would be useful to you in finding a happy relationship. For instance:

- Lasting relationships begin every day.
- Everyone deserves a good relationship.
- People like me find love all the time.
- There are plenty of potential partners out there.
- It is possible to have a great job, lots of success and a strong relationship, too.

Use any of these plus some that you create yourself. Now take your new beliefs and learn them by heart. Repeat them to yourself as often as you can, especially when you find your thoughts heading towards your former negative beliefs.

Choose to believe that a great relationship is on the way

Day Six

LOOK FOR THE EVIDENCE

Today you're going to begin looking for evidence to back up your newly adopted beliefs. Why? Because we all look for evidence to support our beliefs every single day, without even realizing that this is what we are doing. So if you want to change your beliefs, it's important to look for the right evidence.

For example, your old, negative belief may be:

'You can't have a great job and a happy relationship.'

Without even realizing it, you will have looked for evidence to support this viewpoint – in books, magazines and newspapers; on television and radio; in advertisements and in the things people around you say. Every time you came across a woman with a great relationship but a miserable job, or a great job but no relationship, you'll have thought to yourself: 'Ah, you see – I was right about that.' Your belief will have been cemented in even more deeply.

This is how we support ourselves in what we believe. On top of this, because we want to be right in our beliefs, we often filter out any contradicting evidence. You may have read a story in a newspaper about a woman with a fabulous job but a miserable love life and ignored another story in the same newspaper about a woman with a wonderful job *and* a wonderful relationship.

That's why I want you to look for evidence to support your new beliefs.

Suppose your new belief is:

'You can have it all – a great job and a wonderful man.'

Now begin looking for evidence to support this belief, rather than dismissing it as an exception. Notice stories and examples of women proving this – there are plenty of them around! Write them down or cut out the articles and keep them. You'll soon find that you have collected a substantial bundle of 'evidence'; if you need to shore up your new belief, you can simply run through it for reassurance and validation.

A national newspaper once printed a story saying that it was easier for a woman over the age of 35 to go to the moon than for her to marry. Countless numbers of unmarried women over 35 probably took this to heart and used it to confirm that they would never marry. Yet women over 35 marry ALL THE TIME: there are examples in the newspapers every day. So the statistic, as statistics can be, was misleading. There are always statistics available that you can manipulate to prove anything you want to prove.

Believe what you want to believe and then begin to notice how often your belief is true in the world around you. Build your beliefs by building the evidence that supports them.

The evidence that a great relationship is possible is all around you

Day Seven

CHANGING YOUR PATTERN

Now it's time to identify your relationship pattern, decide how useful it has been to you and what changes you'd like to make.

Everyone who has had relationships has a pattern that they fall into often without being conscious of doing so. This pattern is based on their style of behaviour in and around relationships. Here are some examples:

- You rush into one relationship after another. Each time you think 'This is it!' and feel wonderful, only to decide you were wrong and dump the other person within weeks.
- You are very careful about who you get involved with and so cautious that you hardly trust anyone and take a long, long time to feel comfortable enough to date someone new.
- You just never seem to meet anyone. You can go for long periods without a relationship and most of the time this doesn't bother you too much.
- You always get hurt. Each time you think you've met a decent person, he turns out to be the kind who doesn't want to commit.
- You were so badly burned by a relationship once that you can't face trying again.
- You're critical of everyone who wants to date you. You think they cannot possibly be interesting.
- You have no confidence in yourself and hang around in the background at parties and clubs, assuming that no one will be interested in you.

Is your relationship pattern here? Probably, as almost everyone who's not in a long-term relationship fits one of these patterns. If yours is different, however, just write it down. If identifying it feels hard, think about your past few relationships or near-relationships and ask yourself what happened to make them go wrong.

Now that you know what your pattern is, you can resolve to change it. Think about the qualities and behaviour you'll need in order to establish your new pattern. Do you need to be more trusting, more open, or should you be more cautious and go more slowly? Do you need to say no more often, to get to know someone better before getting involved or to trust your own judgment more?

Decide today that you will establish a new pattern for yourself – one that leads to a healthy, lasting relationship with someone you love and respect.

Your new relationship pattern will bring you love

Day Eight

GREAT SELF-TALK

The time has come to look at the way you talk to yourself about yourself and relationships. What kind of language do you use when you talk inside your head about how your love life is going, what you want from the relationship and about what you have to offer?

Do you put yourself down, use all kinds of critical phrases and imagine that other people are doing a whole lot better than you are? Do you punish yourself for the mistakes you make and constantly tell yourself that you should do things better or perhaps differently? If so, then it is no great surprise that you haven't yet found the love you deserve. Unkind talk – your own as much as others – is demoralizing and diminishes your confidence. How can you walk out through your front door feeling sexy and attractive if you have been busy putting yourself down?

Educators now know that if you want a child to succeed, you must praise that child. Criticism will only create a badly behaved, miserable child. It is absolutely no different when you are an adult! And it makes no difference who is doing the criticizing. A put-down is a put-down, even if you're the only person who ever hears it.

Exercise

To discover how you talk to yourself, spend today noticing everything you say to yourself. Write some of it down, if you can. Catch yourself every time you're having a mental conversation with yourself, whether it is in the bathroom, on the way to work, when walking upstairs, while cooking a meal or when doing the washing up.

- What tone of voice do you use?
- How frequently do you use critical words or phrases?
- How often do you tell yourself that you should have done something better?
- How often do you boss yourself about?
- Do you ever use praise, kind words or a soft tone towards yourself?

The chances are that you've found you're pretty tough on yourself. Most people are critical towards themselves 90 per cent of the time. And that's no fun, is it?

If you want to attract a wonderful relationship into your life, it's time to begin being nice to yourself. The way you talk to yourself is the most important way you can do that. Once you are kind, supportive and understanding towards yourself, you'll be amazed by how quickly you start to feel good about who and what you are. When you feel good about yourself, you smile more and you become instantly more confident and attractive, so that other people will be drawn to you like a magnet.

Here's how to begin talking to yourself in an encouraging way:

- Catch yourself every time you're saying something nasty, bossy or critical to yourself.
- Replace what you're saying with something else that is appreciative, kind and understanding.
- Praise yourself for everything you do well during the day, even little things such as getting to work on time or eating something healthy.
- Smile at yourself every time you pass a mirror.
- Before you go to sleep at night, list all your good points and achievements.

Great self-talk leads to great self-esteem

Day Nine

BACKING YOURSELF

This is the day when all the work you've done so far comes together and you decide that from now on you will back yourself, in every possible way, in finding the relationship you truly want.

All too often we don't really back ourselves at all. We criticize and undermine ourselves and forget to give ourselves support, understanding or a pat on the back when we do well. From now on, however, you're going to be someone who supports herself through thick and thin, who hangs on in there when the going gets tough and who never lets herself down.

How do you back yourself 100 per cent?
By taking these steps:

- Always be your own cheerleader.
- Support yourself in the decisions you make and stand up for yourself when others try to put you down.
- Listen to yourself.
- Decide what your opinion is in any given situation and then respect that opinion as valuable and right for you.
- Trust your judgment.
- Do what feels right for you and trust yourself to know best, even if those around you don't agree.
- Give yourself credit for your achievements, your courage, the effort you put in and the great qualities that you possess.
- Recognize your abilities and talents. You will have many of these – everyone does – and you demonstrate them every day, whether you realize it or not.

Think about situations in which you have backed yourself and trusted your judgment, then think about others in which you haven't. Remember how good it felt to back yourself and promise that you'll never let yourself down again.

Backing yourself 100 per cent is vital to finding a lasting relationship because, in choosing someone to become deeply involved with, you will need to trust yourself implicitly and know that you are capable of doing what's right for you.

If your trust in yourself and your judgment are undermined or destroyed – whether by others or by yourself – how can you know that you've met a worthwhile, trust-worthy partner who will be right for you? Believe in yourself, back yourself and let it be your own good judgment that decides what, and who, is right for you.

Back yourself and know how valuable you really are

Day Ten

USE MAGIC

Today you're going to have fun using the power of magic to support your quest to find the perfect relationship for you. Lovers have used magic throughout history. It can be employed to attract the love you want and to draw into your life the person you can love and who can love you.

You don't believe in magic? That's not a problem, as it works whether you believe in it or not. All you have to be willing to do is to suspend your disbelief and give it a try. Magic is about using universal energy on your behalf, and, as long as the magic you practise is intended for the benefit of all, the universe will cooperate and contrive to bring you what you wish for.

Of course, it's important that you do all the other things necessary to secure the relationship you want. Changing your beliefs, dumping your excuses, summoning the courage to go out into the world and look for the person you want are all vital. But using a little white magic is a great way to back up all your efforts and to add universal energy and power to your personal energy.

Here's a white magic ritual you can practise daily:

Stand beside an open window or door, and cup one of your hands. Look into your cupped palm and visualize yourself with your ideal partner, in a happy relationship. Don't use a specific person, even if there's someone on whom you've got your eye. Simply imagine a warm, loving and attractive person, with his or her arms around you.

Now, with your other hand, pluck an imaginary golden thread from the air above you. Use it to sew your cupped palm, containing your dream, shut.

Grasp the end of the golden thread between the thumb and forefinger of your closed palm. Holding this thread, open your palm and throw your dream up into the sky.

Take the end of the thread that you are still holding, tuck it into your waistband and pat it three times. The universe will receive your dream and, because you still have the end of the thread, will know to whom to send it back ... fulfilled.

Another magic ritual you can try is to write out a description of your ideal partner on a piece of paper, then roll it up and tie it with a red ribbon. When the next full moon comes, bury the rolled-up paper in your back garden (or a flowerpot on a windowsill), while visualizing the love you want.

Use these and any other white magic spells or rituals that you may come across to draw love closer to you. Have fun with them – this magic is meant to be light-hearted and exciting, not gloomy and intense.

Let the power of magic draw love to you

Day Eleven

WATCH WHAT YOU SAY

Now it's time to take notice of the way you talk to other people about your relationships, or lack of them. Do you habitually point out your mistakes and seem gloomy about your chances of finding someone right? If so, it's time to stop.

People believe what you tell them and they feed those beliefs back to you. If you keep telling other people that you just can't find the right person, that you don't really need anyone or that you mess up every relationship you have, then that's what you'll hear, too. All of which will only confirm your negativity and leave you feeling convinced that your chances are hopeless.

Thoughts and words convey energy, either negative or positive. This energy has an effect on everyone around you, so it's vital that you give out positive energy. Life often gives you what you ask for. What you talk about and think about is what you're asking life for. Always be careful of what you think and say, as it tends to be what you'll get.

Try this checklist. When you're talking to friends about relationships, do you say any of the following?

- **I'm hopeless at relationships.**
- **I always pick people who hurt me.**
- **I just know I'm heading for another disaster.**
- **I have really bad judgment when it comes to men.**
- **I don't understand what I do wrong.**
- **I'm afraid to try again.**
- **It would be nice to meet someone, but I'm not bothered if I don't.**
- **I'm just too choosy, I guess.**
- **Why aren't there any decent men around?**
- **All men are creeps (or all women hate men).**

Note the phrases that sound familiar and add any more that you regularly use. These are the messages you've been sending out to your friends and to life about what you want!

Now think about the message you'd really like to be giving out. What is it that you truly want? Try some of the following statements:

- I'd love to meet someone genuinely nice.
- I feel sure that my next relationship will work out.
- I'm ready for a great relationship.
- There are lots of lovely, available men out there.
- I've learned a great deal from my past mistakes.
- Life's great, and it will be even better when I have a really good relationship.
- Being hurt will never put me off trying again.
- I have a feeling that I'm going to meet someone very soon.
- Having a wonderful relationship is extremely important to me.

Pick the ones that feel right, add your own and use them – frequently. The people around you – and life – will hear what you want and it will soon arrive on your doorstep.

Be brave and talk about the relationship you really want

Day Twelve

SEEK OUT SUPPORTERS

Right, this is it. It's time to think about the people you spend the most time with and how much they support you in finding the relationship you want and deserve.

All the effort you're making and all the backing you're giving yourself will be useless if you're spending a lot of time with people who undermine or discourage you. This can often be so subtle that it's difficult to spot. Friends and family may be well meaning in the things they say, but they can still leave you feeling miserable, however unintentionally. Sometimes, too, people aren't well meaning. They're simply jealous or unhappy, and they dump these feelings onto you by putting you down.

Watch out for:

- People who sympathize with you yet at the same time agree that you're not likely to find relationship happiness.
- People who tell you that no one would ever love or accept you as you are.
- People who treat you like a loser in love and joke about it.
- People who leave you feeling criticized or undermined, even if you're not exactly sure why.
- People who are generally negative and gloomy.

If there are people like this in your life, make a decision to spend less time with them while you're looking for a relationship. Back away gently, and keep contact to a minimum. When you do see them, don't talk about relationships.

Instead, look out for:

- People who are warm and enthusiastic about your chances of finding real love.
- People who encourage and support you in genuine ways.
- People who are positive in their outlook on life.
- People who you feel really like and appreciate you.
- People who don't consider you a threat to their own relationships or treat you as a fifth wheel.

Think about people you know who are like this and how much contact you have with them. Do you need to strengthen your relationships with supportive people? If so, make the first move RIGHT NOW. Call and arrange to see a friend like this, ask someone supportive out for a drink, or talk to an old friend whom you haven't seen for a while. Put your energy into the people who support you.

Make sure that you spend as much time as possible with people like this and really enjoy their support and encouragement. These are the people to trust with your hopes and dreams, and to confide in when you need to talk.

Good people leave you feeling good

Day Thirteen

YOUR SHOPPING LIST

Prepare to have fun. Today you're going to draw up a shopping list of all the qualities you'd like in a perfect partner. You can indulge yourself totally, get as carried away as you want and put absolutely anything on your list – no matter how outrageous, insignificant or hilarious it may be.

But there's a serious side to this, too. Until you have a really clear idea of who your ultimate partner would be, you will never be able to judge whether potential partners you meet come close to this ideal, or are on the right track. Once you know exactly what you want, you'll be able to decide, very quickly, whether it's worth pursuing possible relationships that come your way.

I'm not suggesting that only your ideal in every respect will do. Like everyone else in the world, you'll need to compromise on some points. It will be up to you, however, to decide where you will compromise and where you won't, what truly matters and what you can overlook or let go.

Exercise

So get yourself a pen and a notebook and settle down for half an hour on your own. It's tempting to do this one with friends and have a laugh. Don't. They'll distract you and make suggestions, and this needs to come from you and you alone. After all, you're the one who is going to be with this person. Write the following headings:

- Character
- Qualities
- Looks
- Habits
- Beliefs
- Skills and Talents
- Family and Friends
- Hopes and Dreams

Now make a list under each heading. Put down only things that matter to you, but be honest about what matters. Don't dismiss anything as too trivial. If you hate smoking, then it's fine to put 'nonsmoker' on your list of requirements.

Here are some ideas to begin with:

Character: Is your ideal partner quiet and thoughtful, or outgoing and chatty? Is this person hard-working and ambitious, or easy-going and happy with a job that simply pays the bills. You'll have grasped the idea – now carry on from here.
Qualities: Which qualities do you value in another person and why do they matter to you? Do they include honesty, loyalty, courage, determination and humour?
Looks: Is he tall or short; blond, red-haired or dark; fat or thin; blue-, brown- or green-eyed? Include any physical characteristics that you find attractive and sexy.
Habits: What habits do you like and which ones drive you crazy? Do you want someone who leaves clothes strewn around the house? Or a tidiness fanatic? This is your chance to come clean!
Beliefs: Do you want someone who believes in being faithful? In working through problems? In talking over his worries? Do you want someone with spiritual beliefs? Think of the beliefs you'd want a partner to share with you.
Skills and Talents: Do you want a great cook? A do-it-yourself expert? A scuba diver? Someone who speaks six languages or loves rock climbing?
Family and Friends: Is your ideal partner close to his family? Does he see them often? Does this person have lots of friends or just a few special ones? How will you fit in with the other people in your partner's life?
Hopes and Dreams: In some crucial areas, your partner's hopes and dreams need to match yours. Do you both want children? Do you want to live in the city or the country? Are you both ambitious or would you rather only one of you were?

When you've finished, mark the three most important items under each heading. These will form the basis of your mental checklist, the one you'll carry with you whenever you're meeting potential partners.

Know what you want and you will be certain to find it

Day Fourteen

WHAT CAN YOU OFFER?

Now you have reached the point where it is necessary to take a long, hard look at yourself and what you've got to offer in order to make your relationship really great. You're sure about what you want in a partner. You've thought hard about the vital qualities that will attract you and that you will value. But what will your future partner be attracted to in you and value most? What will make this person feel you're very special, and that he can trust and respect you?

To build a truly successful relationship, it's important that you share your basic values and beliefs, and that you live by the same code. In other words, if you want someone who's going to be faithful, honest, open and committed, you've got to be those things, too.

Of course, there will be differences between you, things that you love in each other and that you don't share. For instance, your partner may be very laid back, while you're more of a perfectionist. He may love being outdoors, while you'd rather curl up indoors with a good book. This kind of difference is fine, as long as it's something on which you can compromise. But there's no way to compromise on loyalty, honesty and commitment.

Exercise

Look at the qualities you put on your shopping list for your ideal partner (see pages 38–9). How many of those same qualities do you believe you possess yourself? How many have you shown in your previous relationships or in your life in general?

For instance, if you decided that you want someone faithful, understanding, open about their feelings and willing to share themselves and their lives, are you willing to behave in the same way?

Set about cultivating in yourself the qualities you want in someone else. Think hard about what they mean and what they entail. Being open about your feelings, for example, can be painful and difficult at times. If this is important to you, practise it whenever an opportunity comes along.

Also consider the qualities you do have and think of ones you need to develop or learn. Keep a mental list of the qualities you value most and check with yourself regularly to see whether you're practising them. Keep going until they become a part of you, as deeply ingrained as any habit you have without needing to think about it. Promise yourself that you will demonstrate, every single day, all the qualities that you admire and want to have – starting today.

When it comes to personal qualities, like will attract like

Day Fifteen

BE FABULOUSLY ATTRACTIVE

Today you're going to have fun. This is the day when you become fabulously attractive and begin to attract other people to you like moths to a flame.

Becoming fabulously attractive has nothing at all to do with your looks. Of course, some people are naturally pretty or even beautiful, but even these people don't always attract others to them. In fact, many great beauties come across as quite cold and distant. Being fabulously attractive is a quality that anyone can have. It comes from deep inside and simply shines out of the people who have it.

We all know one or two people who are like this. People who light up a room, who are always surrounded by others and who are invited to everything because they're confident and fun to be with. People who are often described as beautiful but who, when you look closely, may not be conventionally beautiful at all.

These people have charisma by the truckload. And charisma – the ability to attract others effortlessly – is something you can cultivate and learn in a very short space of time.

How to be fabulously attractive:

Always look after yourself. Personal grooming is important. Take the trouble to do your hair, nails and make-up carefully and to exercise and eat healthily. Doing these things is a way of cherishing yourself. And when you cherish yourself, you feel good about yourself.

Always wear something you feel good in – throw out anything that doesn't make you feel that you look great. If you go out wearing clothes you don't like, you can't feel attractive. Gorgeous clothes make you feel instantly gorgeous.

Talk to yourself as though you are the most attractive person you know. Tell yourself that you look stunning, compliment yourself often and give yourself a sexy smile every time you pass a mirror.

Smile, often, when you're with other people. Practise smiling warmly at strangers – you'll be surprised how often they smile back. A smile equals instant attraction.

Relax. Nothing is more off-putting than a tense, stressed, anxious person. Someone who's relaxed, who behaves as though life is easy and fun, is fabulously attractive.

Imagine a deep well of beauty inside you, at the very core of who you are, and picture it spreading through you, then flowing out to the rest of the world. It is an intrinsic part of you, going with you wherever you go and making you fabulously attractive to anyone you meet.

Practise confidence, the most attractive quality of all. Truly confident people are comfortable with themselves, they handle power easily, they feel no need to impress or show off, they laugh at their mistakes while learning from them, they respect and value others and they feel good about who they are.

Think of people or public figures you admire who are self-assured and present well, and learn from them.

From today you are truly fabulously attractive

Day Sixteen

SPOIL YOURSELF

It is time to spoil yourself and make yourself feel truly special and wonderful. You're already taking the steps to feel fabulously attractive. Well, spoiling yourself is the next step. You deserve to feel wonderful about yourself, all the time. To feel wonderful you need to be pampered, nurtured and utterly spoiled. Who better to do this than you, as you know exactly what will make you feel fantastic?

This step is an important part of finding a lasting, fulfilling relationship. It is important not only because it will help you to feel good about yourself, but also because in a great relationship lovers love to spoil each other, to make each other feel great and to give each other treats. If you're going to find someone who will do this for you, you need to know exactly what it is that you would like him to do.

It is a universal truth that what you focus on grows. Whatever you are thinking about, believing in and putting your energy into is what you will get. So spoiling yourself, finding out which treats you most love and want from a partner, is where you need to put your focus right now.

Are you thinking that you never meet anyone who wants to spoil you and make you feel loved and gorgeous? Are you imagining that you never will? Stop right now! Believe it or not, most men are more than happy to spoil the women they love and to give them whatever makes them feel good. They just need to know what that is and to feel loved themselves in order to be loving.

Be loving towards yourself now and you'll find it easier to be loving towards your partner when you get together. Offer yourself fun, tenderness and pampering, and you'll be able to offer them to him, too. He will love this and return the attention to you. Here's what I want you to do:

Choose five things that make you feel absolutely wonderful and do them all today.

Here are some ideas:

- Take a long, hot, perfumed bath by candlelight.
- Give yourself a sensual foot massage.
- Curl up for an hour with a magazine or a good book.
- Give yourself a manicure or facial.
- Go for a long walk in the park/woods/beside the sea.
- Listen to your favourite music.
- Give yourself some flowers.
- Buy yourself silky underwear.
- Go to an exercise class.

Choose from this list and add your own ideas. Then, really enjoy giving yourself these treats. Take your time, relax and feel spoiled and good about yourself.

You deserve to be loved, cherished and spoiled

Day Seventeen

ESTABLISH YOUR RULES

Today it's time to choose your dating rules. This is a vital step, as it means that when you begin dating you will have already decided exactly what you will and won't do, what works for you and what is ok by you. Doing this will help you and the person you're dating to know exactly where you stand, what kind of person you are and whether or not you're going to hit it off together. It will save you time, and potential upset and heartbreak. If your date likes to do things very differently from you, it's probably better to stop right there, rather than allow matters to go any further.

Rules are the same as boundaries. Laying down a boundary lets the other person know just how far you'll go, in any situation, and shows firmly and politely that there's no point in pushing you any further.

First of all, think about the dating rules you've been using so far. Even if you haven't been aware of them, you'll certainly have a few.

How much alcohol do you drink? Who decides where you're going? Do you prefer bars, restaurants, clubs or films? Do you kiss or have sex on the first date or not for months? Do you expect him to pay or always pay for yourself? Do you invite him back to your place or wait for him to invite you to his? And so on.

Now think about which of your current rules work for you and which don't. Are there any that leave you feeling a little uncomfortable, under pressure or unsafe? Are there some that keep you at arm's length and make you seem too remote?

Exercise

Get a pen and a piece of paper and write a list of your new dating rules. Choose rules that you feel good about and know you'll be able to stick to. Here are some basic guidelines:

Alcohol: It's never a good idea to get drunk or to be out of control. How many drinks can you have before you need to stop? Know your limit, stick to it and don't let anyone pressure you to drink more.

Sex: It's always wise to wait until you know someone before having sex with them. Once you've had sex with someone, you feel under pressure (from yourself) to embark on a relationship. When you dig a little deeper, however, you may find that you don't even like the person. So give yourself at least a month or ten dates before deciding to have sex.

Money: Paying your share is a sensible approach. This doesn't necessarily mean splitting the bill in half every time you go out. It may be that you buy the drinks and the other person buys the meal. Paying your share is important, as it makes it easier for you to make decisions and take responsibility for what you do and what happens.

Once you've set your dating rules, learn them by heart and make a promise to yourself to stick to them. You'll enjoy yourself more, feel better about yourself and be able to let any man you date know just how you like to do things.

Clever girls have dating rules

Day Eighteen

MEETING PEOPLE

Having identified the kind of person you want to meet, you now need to decide how you want to meet them. So many people wait to meet someone wonderful without thinking about where or how this is likely to happen.

They imagine they'll just bump into him at the bus stop, sit next to him on the train or start chatting in the supermarket queue. Well, these things do happen from time to time, and maybe you will meet the person with whom you'll spend your life this way. But probably not, so putting in a little effort is well worth while.

Think about what kind of person you are and what you like doing. If you love clubbing, big crowds, loud music and dancing, you probably won't want to meet someone whose idea of heaven is a quiet night at home. Equally, if you love staying in, watching television, romantic dinners for two and intimate conversation, there's not much point in getting together with someone keen on partying every night. You need to meet someone whose social style is pretty similar to your own, otherwise you may end up never seeing each other! So identifying your style is the first step.

If you love going out to places where there are lots of people, it's going to be fairly easy to meet new people. But the drawback of big, noisy places is that it can be difficult to talk and strangers can jump into relationships without getting to know each other properly first. On the other hand, if you're the stay-at-home type, it's difficult to meet new people at all.

Work is an important factor here. Do you have a job in which you often meet new people and there are plenty of possible partners around? Lots of people meet their partners at work, so the right kind of job can offer good opportunities. But even if you work alone, with women only or in a tiny firm, don't worry because there are plenty of other ways to meet prospective partners.

Here are some possible ways:

- At parties.
- Through advertisements in magazines and newspapers.
- In pubs and wine bars.
- Through sports and health clubs.
- Through activities – anything from dancing classes to wine-tasting.
- Over the Internet.

Think about the ways in which you'd like to meet someone and how these fit with your lifestyle and social style. Are you willing to make changes, free up more time, put in the effort? If so, it's time for the most vital step of all – taking action.

Every new person you meet draws you a step closer to meeting the love of your life

Day Nineteen

TAKE ACTION

Today is the day for taking action! You've got the self-belief, you know who and what you want and you know, without a doubt, that you can bring whatever you want into your life. That's why it's time to go for it!

Action is the key to change: it's the key to having what you want in life and without it even the best beliefs in the world won't carry you far. Action means following up your words and beliefs with deeds, it means doing whatever you need to and proving to yourself that you are serious about what you want.

Action takes courage, willpower and trust. You need courage to do things differently, to stick your neck out and take a risk, and to cope with change. You need willpower to see your actions through, no matter how scary that is, and to hang in there through the tough times. You need trust because it means that you know, with absolute certainty, that what you want and deserve will come to you if you go for it.

So what action do you need to take today?

Here are some of the possibilities:

- Put an advertisement for the man of your dreams in a newspaper or magazine.
- Join a dating agency or an Internet dating site.
- Organize a party and ask guests to bring an unattached man they know.
- Chat up someone you like the look of.
- Invite a man you find attractive out on a date.
- Sign up for an evening class that interests you – make sure that it's something sexy that men would do, too. Forget upholstery or needlecraft; go for cookery or wine-tasting instead.
- Tell friends that you'd like to meet new men and ask them for introductions.

- Join the gym and go at a time when lots of men are working out.
- Arrange a night out with a couple of friends at a wine bar or pub in an interesting part of town.

You get the idea! Why not do all of these things, then try some more of your own as well. The point is to put lots of energy into doing whatever may lead to meeting someone wonderful. Don't stop at one or two things: be brave, be bold and give yourself plenty of options.

Of course, it doesn't make sense to do anything you won't enjoy. Pick things that will give you a buzz, be fun, teach you something new, get you fit or improve your social life. You can have a great time on the way to fulfilling your goal.

When you take action, you reap rewards

Day Twenty

ASK FOR WHAT YOU WANT

Crunch time. I want you to be prepared to ask, loud and clear, for what you want. When it comes to finding a partner, one of the best ways is by placing an advertisement in the dating column of a newspaper or magazine, or by joining a dating agency.

I bet you passed quickly over these two options on page 52. Most people's reaction is: I couldn't possibly do that because ...

- It's for losers.
- I'm not that desperate.
- I'd just be too embarrassed.

Thousands of people meet partners in one of these ways. Lots of well-adjusted, interesting, clever, good-looking and fun people look for commitment through advertisements and agencies. Why? Because it's straightforward, it opens up your choices and it enables you to meet people you'd never normally meet. It also allows you to choose exactly who you want to meet and who you don't.

So take the plunge and give one of them a try. Asking for what you want, with courage and conviction, will leave you glowing with confidence. And it may work! Statistics show that the most successful advertisements are those placed by women.

Here are some tips:

If you choose advertising, put your advertisement in a newspaper or magazine you like. There's no point in selecting an old (or young) fogey's newspaper if you don't want an old (or young) fogey. Almost all newspapers run dating columns, and lots of magazines – especially listings magazines – do, too.

Be honest. If you want a loving partner who's not afraid of commitment, say so. A lot of men want the same. If you sound too jokey, you'll attract people who'll waste your time.

Think about whether you'd like written replies, rather than telephone messages. Letters give you time to think and often tell you more about the writer.

Reject anyone who sounds much too old or young, or says something in his letter or message which you don't like or which doesn't fit with who you are and what you want.

Give people a chance if they sound shy, nervous or serious. It takes courage to answer an advertisement. You can always find out more over the phone, or meet for an hour.

If you prefer an agency, pick one you can afford that operates near you and caters for people like you. There are agencies for everyone – single parents, divorced people, older people, young people, professionals and students. Do some research first.

As with advertisements, be generous at the beginning. People can seem strained and awkward in this kind of situation but be very different once they're at ease.

At the very least, placing an advertisement or joining an agency will add to your choice of partners. And that's the idea – to meet a variety of people, as eventually one of them will be the person you'll fall in love with.

Ask for what you want and you will get it

Day Twenty-One

PREPARING TO DATE

If you've followed the plan so far, very soon you'll be going on dates – lots of them. Think of this as the chance to have heaps of fun, meet new people, go to exciting places and enjoy yourself. Don't be tempted to bypass the dating stage and plunge straight into a relationship, even if you think you've met your ideal partner. The odds are that the first, second or third date won't be THE one. So be prepared to meet lots of people – and give yourself lots of choice.

Dating is an essential preliminary stage before you settle into a relationship. It's a chance to have a good time while fine-tuning your ability to distinguish relationship potential from relationship no-nos. If dating is going to be a big success, you need to prepare. So today's task is to make sure you're absolutely ready for dating to begin.

Your pre-dating checklist

1 Line up petcare or childcare if you need it. Make sure you have someone reliable to call on at short notice. 'I can't get a babysitter' is a deadly dull dating excuse. 'I can't leave my cat on his own' is worse.

Line up a friend, too – not to go with you (that's tacky and a recipe for disaster), but to know where you are and who you're with if you go on any blind dates.

2 Clear your diary. This is especially important if you're a workaholic. It's time to put yourself and your love life first. Make sure you've got several days a week free for dates. When potential dates come along, you don't want to be booking them for a month ahead – you could seem overbusy, wary or unenthusiastic, and no one will wait around long enough to find out how wonderful you really are.

3 Think of interesting venues that you'd be comfortable going to with new dates. If you're the one who suggests where you meet, it gives you an instant advantage and makes you sound like someone who goes out a lot, whether you actually do or not. Suggest places that are easy to get to, fun to be in, attractive and popular, but not so busy or loud that you can't get comfortable or hear yourself speak. When you are on a date, you want to be able to sit, talk, stop talking without a deadly silence descending and get home easily.

If you don't know any suitable places, ask friends, look around your area, check out places you pass by and generally do some research.

4 Sort out your wardrobe. Dating crisis number one is: 'I don't know what to wear.' Don't panic – this goes for men, too. Avoid it by working out what you feel great in right now. Go and look through your clothes. If there's nothing you think is suitable for the occasion, it's time to go shopping. If there's something you feel comfortable and at ease in, yet still sexy and attractive, great – keep it ready.

Checklist completed?

You're ready to begin dating!

Day Twenty-Two

DATING

So you've cleared the way, lined up the dates, sorted out your wardrobe and you're all set to go. Fantastic. Today it's time to think about how you want your dates to go and what will make you feel relaxed and confident when dating someone you don't know well – or at all!

First of all remember what a date is – and isn't:

It is: An opportunity to get to know someone, to decide whether you'd like to see him again, to let someone get to know you, to share drinks and food and conversation, and to forget about the routine things in life and enjoy yourself.

It's not: A lifetime's contract, a promise to have sex, a bargaining forum (food for sex), a chore, an ordeal, a meeting of souls or the chance for a few free drinks.

The most important thing you can do on a date is to treat the person you're with as a human being. Remember that he's probably nervous, he's likely to have made an effort, he also wants it to work out and he may be trying a bit too hard to impress you. So give him a chance.

If you don't know what to talk about, ask him about himself – his life, his interests, his family. Almost everyone loves to talk about themselves. If he won't talk about himself or is evasive and vague, take it as a possible warning sign, as it may mean that he keeps secrets, he's holding back or he's going to be hard work.

Other warning signs to watch out for include:

- **He talks about himself nonstop.**
- **He boasts a lot.**
- **He has no sense of humour.**

Warning signs mean you should think twice about a second date, although don't rule it out if a warning sign is counterbalanced by something you really like about him (apart from looks). But be aware that warning signs often indicate traits that would be difficult to put up with in the long run. It may be better to say no now, rather than later.

Hot dating tip: The most valuable thing you can take on a date is a smile – preferably a warm, sexy one. Polish yours and keep it ready.

Remember, a date that doesn't work out simply leaves an opening for a date with someone else. A date that does work out and leads to another date is exciting enough to be worth all the effort and all the nerves.

Dating is the route to finding real love

Day Twenty-Three

BEWARE OF THUNDERBOLTS

The more people you meet, the more dates you can go on. Of course, you may meet the right person straight away. It is more likely, however, that you will have to go out with a few people before you find the one who is right for you.

Some of the people you date may seem wrong from the outset. Still, think about why they seem wrong before you decide against a second date. If the reason is something that gets on your nerves and is unlikely to change, such as arrogance, sarcasm or self-obsession, then fine, don't go back there! If you like the person, however, but don't feel any particular chemistry, be willing to see him again and let the liking deepen. You may be surprised by what happens.

In these days of fast pace and fast living, we have come to expect that everything will happen fast. If instant attraction isn't there, we dismiss someone. In most strong, happy relationships, though, love and attraction have grown, inch by inch.

In fact the people we feel instantly attracted to can often be the ones to avoid. If you have a history of falling for men at once, only to be disappointed, don't let yourself do it again. Instant attraction is fun – the buzz is exciting, the promise enormous. But then, pretty soon afterwards, so is the disappointment. That's why today I want you to beware of thunderbolts. When mutual attraction hits us like a thunderbolt, it's often disastrous.

Why? Because when that happens it's not the person to whom we are attracted. How can it be? We don't really know them. It's simply that this person has triggered something in us, a recognition, usually connected to the past.

For instance, suppose Jane's father was a charming, irresponsible man who could never commit or stay in a relationship and who wasn't around much when Jane was young. As his child, however, she loved him and thought he was perfect. Even when she grew up and knew he wasn't perfect, she still loved him and longed for his interest and attention.

When she started having relationships with men, she chose partners just like her father. Of course, she never thought they'd be like him – some of them seemed very different at first. But there was always an instant attraction and Jane didn't wait to find out what they were really like before getting involved. The same pattern always re-emerged eventually: her partners, just like her father, left her.

If you find yourself attracted to someone immediately, then go very, very slowly. Promise yourself lots of time to get to know this person. Stand back a little, put the attraction aside and think about what he is really like. It may be that you need to bypass this kind of attraction in order to find the person who is right for you. Attraction that has grown more slowly generally lasts much longer.

The bigger the thunderbolt, the more likely the disaster

Day Twenty-Four

GO FOR GOLD

Today is the day to remember that nothing but the best will do for you. Finding love is not about settling for anyone who comes along, or even for someone who seems halfway right. It's about finding someone who is worthy of the love you have to give, and that means someone who is really special in every way – pure gold. That's why I want you to go for gold and to make this your motto in your search for love.

It's easy to come across people who are the equivalent of fool's gold. In other words, they appear to be wonderful, until you look a little deeper. That's why it's so crucial to take your time in getting to know someone and to find out what kind of person he really is. Surface glitz is attractive and charm is magnetic, but lasting relationships need more than these. Be aware that people who make a dazzling first impression can prove very different in the long term.

Women are often attracted to the kind of men who treat them badly, who don't call, who let them down, ignore them, criticize them or hurt them. So many women say: 'I don't know why I always go for mean men.' Well, here are some reasons:

- **Mean men can seem exciting at first.**
- **They seem more of a challenge.**
- **Women who like mean men believe, deep down, that they don't deserve anyone better and that the choice is a mean man or no one at all.**

The same women often justify their choice by saying that nice men are boring. Of course, there are pleasant men who are also bland and dull. Men who are honest, open, not afraid of commitment, generous and loving, however, are not boring. They're fantastic! They make better lovers, better partners and better friends than the mean sort ever will. They're the kind of man you need to look for if you want a good, long-term relationship.

Who would choose suffering over being loved and made to feel cherished? Only a woman who doesn't know her own worth.

Think of Bridget Jones and the two men she had to choose between. One seemed sexy and exciting, the other dull and boring. But who came through? Mr Dull and Boring, who turned out to be more sexy and exciting than the other guy could ever hope to be. Ultimately, the seemingly sexy one turned out to be a self-obsessed, immature waste of time.

If you believe that you're pure gold and that any man would be lucky to be with you, you'll go for a man who's pure gold himself. And that means someone worthy of you.

Go for gold – you deserve the best

Day Twenty-Five

IGNORE SETBACKS

Now it's time to look at the way you deal with problems and setbacks. In finding the right relationship for you, there will inevitably be the occasional hiccup. Things go wrong from time to time – that's part of life. The important thing is how you deal with them. You can take them to heart, worry, agonize and feel depressed about it. Or you can feel temporarily disappointed, then carry right on with your plan.

What can go wrong? Here are some possible examples:

- You are stood up on a date.
- You really like someone, but he doesn't want to see you again.
- He says he'll call, but doesn't.
- You think he's the one, rush into a relationship and then get dumped – he only wanted a fling.
- You've met one or two nice men, but they don't ask you out.
- You just can't find the courage to go on a blind date.
- You made a complete fool of yourself by doing something that embarrassed both you and your date.

There are plenty of other possible hiccups. I'm sure you can come up with a few! So what should you do when something like this happens? Here's what:

- Give yourself up to an hour to feel really disappointed, annoyed, idiotic or hurt.
- After the hour is up, THAT'S IT. Simply refuse to dwell on it or to indulge those unhappy feelings any more.
- Remind yourself that if he behaved badly he's not worth a second of your time or a moment of your energy and interest.
- Be glad that you found out sooner rather than later that he's not good enough for you.
- Arrange to see a good friend and LAUGH with her about what happened. Don't tell it like a sad story, but as a funny one. Don't spend too long on it – ten minutes is enough, and refuse to analyse the situation. Instead, move on to talking about something else.

- **Do something straight away to move you on your way towards your goal. Arrange another date, call another man, plan another party, write out another advertisement – whatever's next on the list.**

This is how you prove that you can take disappointment lightly – it's a skill you'll need all your life. Ok, so you were let down or made an idiot of yourself. So what? So on to better things, that's what. Keep your disappointments small – don't let them grow by focusing on them.

Remember that every person in a successful relationship will have experienced disappointments along the way. Some of them will have had many. You can either give in or you can laugh in the face of disappointment and get back out there!

Take setbacks lightly and carry straight on

Day Twenty-Six

TAKE YOUR TIME

Today I want you to focus on the importance of taking your time and going slowly into a relationship. Why? Because there's a simple truth that applies to 99 per cent of relationships:

The faster you go in, the more likely it is to end quickly.

We tend to go into relationships at the same speed we come out of them. If you rush into a relationship, starry-eyed and convinced that because a man is gorgeous he's perfect for you and longing to commit, you lose your sense of balance. Speed, like drink, impairs the judgment. And the further in you get, the more you feel you have to make it work, even if you discover something you don't like or trust about him.

On the other hand, progressing slowly – getting to know someone, dating, holding hands, holding back until you feel more certain – has everything going for it. You never lose your sense of judgment, so you can see, far more clearly, what this person is really like.

By taking your time you may learn things that may make you think twice about going deeper into a relationship with him. For instance, he might be an alcoholic, he might be a serial womanizer, he might be hung up on his ex and not emotionally free, he might be about to be fired, he might be too attached to his parents, he might not have any friends or he might be unreliable and irresponsible. All these are things you can only find out over time, as they're not the sort of things you could detect about most people on a first or second date.

When you rush in, you get all of the fun part over with very fast. The buzz, the heat, the first touch, the first kiss and so on ... You can have more fun when you take the relationship slowly. Spin it out and add anticipation to the joy of being around someone who attracts and excites you.

Ending it is easier when you go slowly. When you haven't dived in deep, it's much easier to walk away if something begins to feel wrong. This is important, as the more time you spend with someone who isn't right, the longer you put off being with someone who is.

If you find yourself tempted to rush in fast (and almost everyone has rushed in, at some point), slow yourself down by:

- Letting a week pass before you go on another date.
- Reading this page to yourself again.
- Reminding yourself that, if he's worth knowing, he'll be glad that you want to get to know the real him.
- Making an agreement with a friend that you won't get deeply involved in less than six weeks, and report back regularly.
- Telling him at the outset that you don't want to rush into anything – he'll be intrigued.

Take your time and reap the rewards

Day Twenty-Seven

STAY OPEN

It's time to remind yourself to stay open to all the possibilities that dating and meeting new men can bring. This means being aware of danger signs as well as being aware of potential. It means being choosy, but not too choosy.

In other words, while you're dating, use your intuition and judgment to decide who might be worth getting to know a little more and who is a definite no-no. Here are some examples to guide you:

Danger signs

He drinks heavily or he takes drugs

Remember that it's impossible to get to know someone who's drunk or taking drugs. Alcohol and drugs mask feelings and alter behaviour.

He has no money

This could be a regular state for him, and you might end up poorer because of it.

He never stops joking

Men with this tendency are often insecure and trying to cover up that insecurity. The flip side of a joker can be someone who is dark and depressing.

He has lots of mates or acquaintances, but no real friends

Someone like this finds genuine relationships difficult. He prefers to keep things at a superficial level, an attribute you may later grow to hate.

He shows off

Boasting is boring and another sign of insecurity.

He takes no real interest in you

If he finds you attractive, but can't be bothered to ask about you or remember things you've told him about yourself, he considers this a short-term affair.

He's thoughtless towards you

He leaves you to follow him into places, leaves you nursing a drink while he chats to friends, assumes you don't want to eat if he doesn't – this kind of attitude tends to get worse with time, not better.

He has never found a job he likes

A lot of self-esteem, especially for men, is tied up with work. If he hates his job, he probably doesn't feel good about himself.

Encouraging signs

- He calls when he says he'll call.
- He is genuinely interested in what you have to say.
- He likes his job (or he's changing it).
- He confides in you about what he feels, thinks, dreams of and believes.
- He treats you well and makes you feel good.
- He talks warmly about his close friends.
- He can, at times, be very funny.
- He is generous with his money.
- He's solvent (that is, he meets his financial responsibilities).
- He knows why his past relationships went wrong and he doesn't just blame the women.

Nothing's written in stone. A danger sign doesn't necessarily rule a man out: it only suggests that you need to be very careful and keep your eyes open. Equally, a couple of encouraging signs doesn't mean he's right for you in every way.

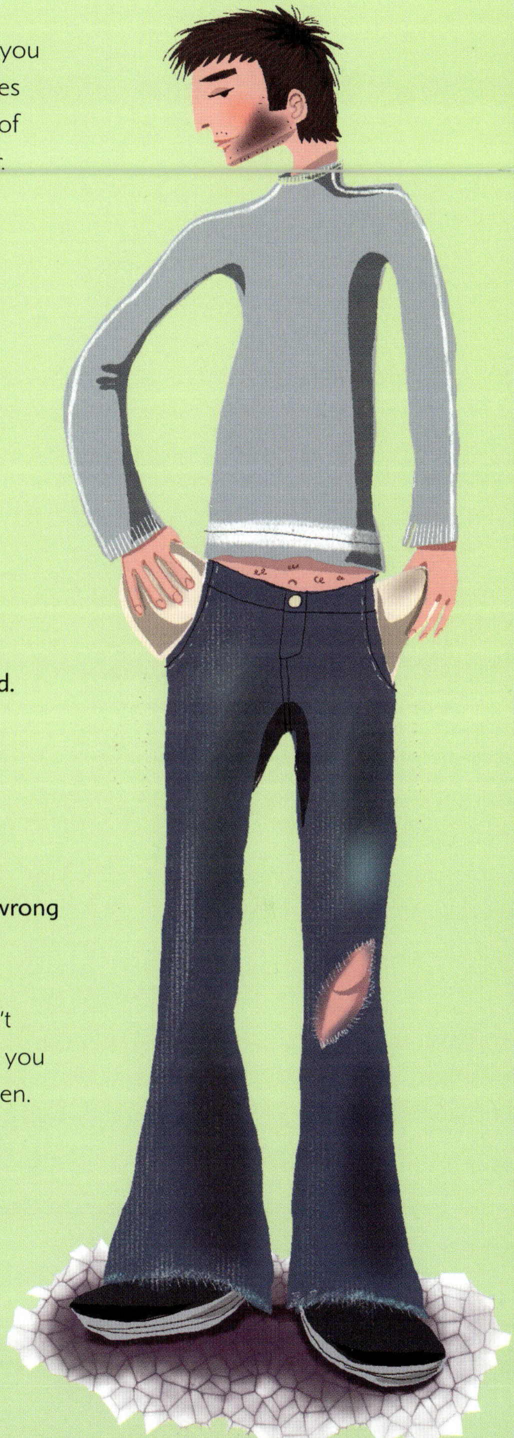

Stay open to the possibilities and trust yourself

Day Twenty-Eight

STAY ON TRACK

Today's the day to remind yourself to stay on track and keep going, however much effort this requires.

Finding love means being prepared for hard work. It's not enough to love the idea of falling in love. To find real love you need dedication, determination and courage. You need to be willing to take risks, say no when you have to, say yes even when it's scary and hang on in there even when you feel like giving up. And there are bound to be moments when you feel like giving up, when it would be a lot easier to curl up in front of the television with a box of chocolates and think: 'Oh well, I gave it a shot and it didn't work.' But you want to find love, not settle for excuses, so when you reach that point you're going to finish the chocolates, get up out of your cosy armchair and keep on going.

Exercise

Pick a quiet time to try this keep-going strategy. Make sure there won't be any interruptions, and lie or sit somewhere comfortable with your eyes closed:

Imagine that somewhere out there is a man who is going to make you incredibly happy. A man who understands you, who is strong and caring, who'll hang on in there even on the days when you feel like pushing him away. This man has humour, generosity, compassion and depth. He has energy, he's intelligent, he's interesting and he knows how to work hard. He's also incredibly sexy.

Of course, he's human, he has faults. So have you. There will be days when he irritates you or gets it wrong. On balance, however, the good outweighs the bad by ten to one and you will love him and be loved by him enough to get through absolutely anything together.

On a certain day, which is already in the universal diary, you're going to meet this man. As long as you don't let it pass you by. If you're sitting at home doing nothing, wasting your time with a loser or giving up on love, the day and the man will carry on past you. But if you put your energy, motivation and attention towards this meeting, it will happen, and the day may come much sooner than you think.

You deserve him. You deserve the best. You deserve happiness. So go for it.

Staying on track means being willing to take the next step, even when you really don't want to. It means keeping your goal clearly in mind and knowing that the goal is more important than anything that happens along the way. It means believing, with all your heart, that you will achieve your goal.

If you feel you're sliding off the track, say to yourself:

- I know I can do this.
- I never give up on something I've set out to do.
- I deserve a great person to love and I'm going to find him.
- I've got courage and willpower.
- Every minute of every day I'm getting closer to the love I want.

Stay on track towards the love you deserve

Day Twenty-Nine

REVIEW YOUR PROGRESS

This is the day for taking a good look at exactly what you've done and achieved so far and for deciding whether you need to add or change anything.

First of all, go back through the previous 28 steps and assess how you've done. Did you skip any? Skim over a few? Feel half-hearted about one or two? It's useful to look at this, as the chances are that the ones you most resisted are the ones you most need to do. That's the way life often works. We protest, reassure ourselves and make excuses, but in the end it's usually the things we do our utmost to avoid that we most need to face.

It's worth being honest with yourself and then going back and doing the step or steps that you missed. Being half-hearted won't find you love. Facing up to the things you don't want to deal with will. Whatever you missed will be a vital key in your progress towards love. So don't short-change yourself: give yourself 100 per cent backing by doing every step fully.

In the same way, if there was a step that felt especially good to you and seemed to strike a deep chord, go over it again. Many of the steps will have carried through with you throughout the following days and will have created new beliefs and behaviours that will remain with you.

Once you've reviewed the steps up to this point, look at the action you've taken to meet new men and make dates. Have you been taking action, day in, day out, to do this? If so, how is it going? Are you flagging a little or feeling love is as far away as ever? Or are you full of energy and excitement, and raring to go? If so, great. If you're flagging, however, go back over the early steps in the book to reboost your self-belief and motivation.

Remember that success is a combination of belief and consistent action. A burst of energy that fizzles out won't do it. You need to keep taking action, every day, until you eventually reach your goal. Now is a good time to create an action plan to work with over the coming weeks.

Exercise

Think about the steps you can take, day by day, to move you closer to love. The calls you need to make, the people you need to talk to, the places you need to go to, the self-belief you need to reinforce.

Write out an action plan and keep it in your handbag or somewhere close to you and look at it often. Change it when you need to – the best plans are flexible and can be adapted. Add fresh ideas to your action plan whenever you can and update it whenever you achieve a success.

Make progress every day towards finding love

Day Thirty

CELEBRATE!

You've made it through to the end of the 30 days and now you deserve to celebrate. Celebrating is a way of saying to yourself 'Well done' and of appreciating yourself and your efforts.

Celebrating means hanging out, having fun, feeling good and letting everyone else join in, so it's a good idea to do it often! Here's what you've got to celebrate:

- Your determination.
- Your courage.
- Your willingness to keep going.
- Your ability to have fun.
- Your adventurousness.
- Your humour.
- The steps that you've taken towards finding love.
- The fact that you've found love or that you're about to do so.
- The fact that you're now a GORGEOUS human being.
- All the successes you've already had, no matter how big or small.

How to celebrate? Think about what you most enjoy doing and use it as a way of celebrating. You could:

- Throw a party.
- Invite a few friends over.
- Go out for a meal.
- Buy yourself a bottle of champagne.
- Give yourself a present.
- Dance to music you love.
- Fill your home with flowers.
- Make sexy eye contact with a gorgeous stranger on the way to work.
- Wear an outfit in which you feel fabulous.
- Wear the sexiest lipstick you can find.

Or you could do all of them!

Whatever you do, do it for pure pleasure, with energy and love. Remember that celebrating is a big part of finding love, and that, when you're with the right person, celebrating happens easily and often. So get in practice, know how you love to celebrate and enjoy every moment.

Celebrate the joy of finding real love

A FINAL WORD

Following the steps in this book will have set you on your path towards finding the love you want and deserve. It has given you a blueprint you can continue to work from until you've found that lasting and rewarding love. Even then, it's important that you keep your new beliefs, attitudes and energy, as they'll carry you on to a successful future, building and sustaining your loving relationship.

Never let doubts about reaching your goal get the better of you. Having doubts is just the same as feeling scared. Feeling scared is fine, as long as you carry on anyway. If you stop when you're scared, you are giving in to the belief that what you fear is true.

Remember that what you concentrate on grows, so focus on the positive, the exciting, the wonderful, the joyful and the adventurous. Keep your beliefs strong and clear, and know, in your heart and mind and soul, that love is your right.

Resources

FURTHER READING

Beattie, Melody, **Codependent No More**, Center City, MN, Hazelden, 1996

Bowes, Susan, **Love Spells and Rituals**, New Alresford, Godsfield, 2001

De Angelis, Barbara, **Are You the One for Me?**, London, Thorsons, 1996

Domar, Alice D and Drehrer, Henry, **Self-Nurture: Learning to Care for Yourself**, New York, NY, Viking, 1999

Hardie, Titania, **Love Potions**, London, Quadrille, 2002

Lindenfield, Gael, **Bouncing Back from Heartbreak**, London, Thorsons, 2002

Lindenfield, Gael, **Self-Esteem**, London, Thorsons, 2000

Mellody, Pia, **Facing Love Addiction**, San Francisco, CA, Harper San Francisco, 1992

Norwood, Robin, **Women Who Love Too Much**, New York, NY, Arrow/Random House, 1998

Sher, Barbara and Gottlieb, Amie, **Wishcraft: How to Get What You Really Want**, New York, NY, Ballantine Books, 1986

Temsi, Carolyn and Handley, Caro, **Love Wisdom**, New York, NY, Pocket Books, 1999

WEBSITES

www.ivillage.co.uk

(Plenty of good ideas, support and other women's stories on the relationship channel)

www.oprah.com

(relationships, self-care and sorting out your love life)